I0454431

The Online Marketplace Entrepreneur

Building and Scaling a Successful
E-commerce Platform

Introduction..4
Introduction to Online Marketplaces...........................7
    1.1 Defining an Online Marketplace............................7
    1.2 Role and Importance in E-commerce................. 12
Types of Online Marketplaces..................................... 17
    2.1 B2B (Business to Business)...............................17
    2.2 B2C (Business to Consumer).............................. 21
    2.3 C2C (Consumer to Consumer)........................... 26
    Identifying your Niche and Creating a Unique Value
    Proposition... 30
    3.1 Finding the Perfect Niche....................................30
    3.2 Developing a Unique Value Proposition..............34
Business Model of Online Marketplace........................ 39
    4.1 Various Models to Choose From.........................39
    4.2 Exploring Revenue Streams............................... 43
    4.3 Pricing Strategy That Works............................... 47
Building the Marketplace.. 52
    5.1 Setting Up the Platform.....................................52
    5.2 UI/UX Design for Enhancing User Experience.... 56
    5.3 Legal Aspects to Consider.................................. 60
Marketing and Acquiring Users....................................65
    6.1 Essential Digital Marketing Strategies.................. 65
    6.2 Advertisement and PR...................................... 69
    6.3 Leveraging Social Influencers.............................75
Scaling your Online Marketplace................................. 79
    7.1 Advanced Marketing Strategies for Growth.......... 79
    7.2 Partnering and Strategic Alliances......................83
    7.3 Expanding into New Markets.............................. 88
Overcoming Challenges in Scaling..............................93

8.1 Problem-solving for Common Issues.................... 93

Conclusion.. 99

Introduction

In the digitally powered world we inhabit, e-commerce has permeated every aspect of our lives, steadily usurping traditional retail landscapes and ushering a new era of convenience, efficiency, and global connectivity. Flowing within this e-commerce torrent is a potent current - the online marketplace. It has shown exponential growth and a capacity to overhaul economies on a global scale. The roaring success of titans such as Amazon, eBay, and Alibaba have painted a picture that is both promising and challenging. Amidst this backdrop, the role and journey of an online marketplace entrepreneur emerge as the herald of evolution in modern commerce.

"The Online Marketplace Entrepreneur: Building and Scaling a Successful E-commerce Platform" seeks to guide entrepreneurs on this exhilarating yet daunting path. It peels back the ornate curtain to expose the machinery that propels a successful online marketplace. Of the many entrepreneurs who venture into this field, some turn their humble start-ups into billion-dollar behemoths, whilst others fade into oblivion. What sets them apart? The answer lies in understanding the nuances of online marketplaces, building a reliable platform with a unique value proposition, developing intelligent marketing strategies, and skillfully scaling up the business.

The chapters that follow unravel these aspects in detail, providing keen insights, practical advice, and expert strategies to navigate the path from ideation to success. Whether you're aspiring to launch your start-up, seeking to scale your existing e-commerce platform, or simply intrigued by the realm of online marketplaces, this book offers highly relevant and valuable perspectives.

As the metropolis of online commerce continues to expand, a new breed of entrepreneurs is sculpting its skyline. This book is dedicated to these entrepreneurs—the architects of the digital commercial era. The journey of an online marketplace entrepreneur is not for the faint-hearted; it's for those who dare to make a dent in the universe. If you consider yourself amongst these daring individuals, then this, dear reader, is your roadmap. Let us venture together into the exhilarating world of online marketplaces.

Chapter one

Introduction to Online Marketplaces

1.1 Defining an Online Marketplace

An online marketplace, synonymous with the term e-commerce platform, is a virtual space where sellers and buyers meet, engage, and transact business. It is a digital commercial ecosystem, centralizing the exchange of goods and services from multiple vendors, and presenting them to a wide-ranging consumer base. This virtual aggregation of diverse products and services under one umbrella alleviates the need for individual websites or physical stores, creating a one-stop shopping experience backed by competitive pricing, product variety, and convenience.

Similar to a traditional brick-and-mortar shopping centre, the online marketplace thrives by offering shoppers an array of products and services from multiple vendors, while simultaneously providing businesses the platform to reach a broader audience. However, unlike a physical space, the digital environment transcends geographical boundaries, offering a seamless shopping experience 24/7, from the comfort of one's own home.

The Anatomy of an Online Marketplace

To develop a comprehensive understanding of an online marketplace, it is imperative to dissect its core elements and explore the interactions that shape the virtual ecosystem. An online marketplace typically comprises the following three primary components:

1. Platform: A web-based application or mobile application that serves as the virtual infrastructure

to host a multitude of suppliers and their respective offerings. The platform is designed with a user-centric approach, facilitating easy navigation, a secure payment gateway, and an efficient review and rating system, promoting transparency and trust between the users.

2. Sellers: The diverse group of suppliers, retailers, or manufacturers who showcase and sell their products or services on the platform, bolstering the offerings and competition. The sellers may either be individual entrepreneurs, SMEs (Small and Medium Enterprises), or large corporations. Joining an online marketplace allows them to focus their efforts on product quality and customer service, while the platform's infrastructure simplifies their processes.

3. Buyers: The end consumers of products or services. They reap the benefits of diverse

offerings, competitive prices, and the convenience of shopping from anywhere, at any time. The online marketplace acts as an intermediary, streamlining the transaction between buyers and sellers while ensuring safety and reliability.

Online Marketplace Distinctions

Online marketplaces can be distinguished in several ways, such as by their targeted audiences, features, and purpose. The following are common classifications based on audience type:

1. B2B (Business to Business): These platforms facilitate transactions between businesses, usually involving wholesale trade. Examples include Alibaba, ThomasNet, and Global Sources.

2. B2C (Business to Consumer): Focused on transactions between businesses and individual consumers, these platforms incorporate retail

products and services like Amazon, Walmart, and Target.

3. C2C (Consumer to Consumer): As the name suggests, these platforms facilitate transactions between individual consumers, driven by peer-to-peer sales. eBay, Craigslist, and Facebook Marketplace are prime examples.

In addition to these audience-based distinctions, online marketplaces may also vary concerning their features, such as vertical or horizontal marketplaces. A vertical marketplace concentrates on a specific niche or industry, offering products or services related to a particular sector, such as Etsy for handmade crafts. In comparison, a horizontal marketplace serves a divergent range of products or services, catering to multiple sectors under one platform, like Amazon or eBay.

1.2 Role and Importance in E-commerce

The online marketplace plays a pivotal role in shaping the modern e-commerce landscape, forging an ever-evolving digital ecosystem that continuously redefines how goods and services are exchanged on a global scale. The burgeoning popularity and importance of online marketplaces in the world of e-commerce can be attributed to several key factors, which jointly contribute to the thriving virtual commercial environment.

1. Breaking Geographical Boundaries

   Online marketplaces have eliminated geographical barriers, opening up access to global markets and customers. Sellers are no longer constricted by the limitations of their physical location, transcending boundaries to reach a more extensive consumer base. This increased accessibility to diverse products and services fosters healthy competition and encourages innovation.

Similarly, buyers benefit from the vast selection of products and services available, which may not be accessible in their immediate geographical vicinity. The convenience of comparing prices, features, and reviews from various sellers, within a single platform, simplifies the decision-making process and enhances the overall shopping experience.

2. Economies of Scale

By centralizing multiple vendors within a single platform, online marketplaces facilitate economies of scale. This aggregation reduces the end-to-end distribution costs and time, helping businesses achieve better operational efficiency. High traffic volume and transaction density drive down platform costs per sale, allowing sellers to gain a competitive edge by offering lower prices while still maintaining healthy profit margins.

For the platform itself, the presence of multiple vendors ensures diversified revenue streams, protection from potential price fluctuations, and broader market reach, fostering long-term financial stability and growth.

3. Boosting Smaller Businesses and Local Communities

The affordable entry-points offered by online marketplaces empower small businesses and individual entrepreneurs to venture into digital commerce. Without the need for expensive physical storefronts or the costs associated with creating and maintaining their own e-commerce websites, local businesses and start-ups can tap into a massive customer base, driving growth and development while staying competitive among industry giants.

Moreover, online marketplaces provide a platform for local artisans, craftsmen, and producers to showcase their unique products to the world, preserving cultural heritage and generating economic growth within their communities.

4. Fostering Innovation and Disruption

The competitive environment prevalent within online marketplaces spurs innovation and diversification among businesses looking to establish their unique value proposition. Platform features such as AI-driven recommendations, sophisticated search algorithms, and robust review systems stimulate competition on various fronts, including product quality, pricing, and customer service.

Furthermore, developing technologies like virtual and augmented reality have started to permeate the online marketplace sphere, creating new possibilities and disruptive business models, redefining the e-commerce landscape.

5. Creating a Sustainable E-commerce Ecosystem

The increasing use of data analytics, artificial intelligence, and machine learning in online marketplaces has revolutionized marketing, logistics, and operations, creating a more sustainable, efficient, and eco-friendly e-commerce environment. By offering innovative solutions to tackle logistics, waste reduction, and inventory management, online marketplaces contribute significantly to reducing environmental impact and fostering sustainable practices.

Chapter two

Types of Online Marketplaces

2.1 B2B (Business to Business)

In the varied realm of online marketplaces, B2B, or Business-to-Business platforms, have emerged as a conduit for fostering relationships between businesses, creating a virtual hub for transactions predominantly revolving around wholesale trade, sourcing, procurement, and service provision. By streamlining the traditionally time-consuming and complex process of sourcing, negotiation, and purchase execution, B2B online marketplaces have become an essential cog in the global commerce machine.

For online marketplace entrepreneurs, embracing the opportunities inherent in B2B marketplaces involves a nuanced understanding of the various types within this sector.

1. Wholesale Marketplaces

   Wholesale marketplaces serve as a platform for retailers and other businesses to purchase goods in large quantities, often directly from the manufacturers or certified distributors. The primary benefit of these marketplaces lies in their capacity to offer products at significantly lower prices due to the bulk buying nature of the transactions. Alibaba and DHGate are exemplary platforms within this category.

   As an entrepreneur, venturing into a wholesale marketplace requires effective management of logistics, pricing, and fulfillment strategies to maintain a competitive edge and attract large-scale buyers.

2. Procurement Marketplaces

   Procurement marketplaces, including platforms like SAP Ariba and Coupa, provide businesses with a more organized, efficient, and transparent procurement process. These platforms enable businesses to manage supplier networks, create and manage procurement proposals, establish contract terms, and execute and track orders.

   For an entrepreneur in this arena, maintaining a compelling product or service portfolio, complementing it with seamless service, and building trustworthy relationships with customers prove pivotal.

3. Vertical-specific B2B Marketplaces

   These platforms focus on a specific industry or niche, offering products or services tailored to that particular domain. This specialization allows businesses to source highly specific products or engage services targeted towards their particular needs, ensuring high quality and adherence to industry standards. Examples include Handshake, a B2B platform for the retail industry, and Medibox, a B2B marketplace focusing on the pharmaceutical industry.

Entrepreneurs aspiring to establish a vertical-specific B2B marketplace must obtain a deep understanding of the industry they're servicing, understand its unique needs, challenges, and deliver a highly tailored and compelling value proposition to stand out in the competitive landscape.

4. Service-based B2B Marketplaces

Unlike product-based marketplaces, service-based B2B platforms facilitate the procurement of services rather than physical goods. These platforms connect businesses with service providers spanning diverse domains like marketing, IT, consulting, and HR, amongst others. Upwork and Toptal are prime examples of such platforms.

2.2 B2C (Business to Consumer)

B2C (Business to Consumer) online marketplaces have become a cornerstone of modern retail, bridging the gap between businesses and consumers in the virtual shopping space. These platforms offer a variety of products and services directly to individual consumers, ensuring a seamless and convenient shopping experience.

With the growth in technological advancements and the increased adoption of internet-based shopping, diversified models of B2C marketplaces have emerged, each serving different needs, audiences, and market segments. Understanding the different types of B2C online marketplaces provides crucial insights for aspiring entrepreneurs entering this dynamic sector.

- Generalist Marketplaces

  Generalist marketplaces, such as Amazon and eBay, are platforms offering a wide range of product categories. They serve as virtual department stores, housing myriad brands and product types spanning numerous sectors. Shoppers can find virtually anything, from electronics and clothing to kitchenware and books on these platforms.

  For entrepreneurs seeking to venture into these types of marketplaces, there are opportunities to partake as third-party sellers, supplementing the platform's product offerings and thriving off the high customer traffic levels. However, establishing a notable presence amid the vast competition can be challenging and requires strategic pricing, aggressive marketing, and stellar customer service.

- Specialty Marketplaces

  Specialty marketplaces, such as Zappos or ASOS, focus on specific product categories or sectors like fashion, electronics, or home decor. These marketplaces position themselves as authorities within their niche, offering customers a vast and in-depth range of products within a particular sector.

  Entrepreneurs aiming to launch or join a specialty marketplace need to possess a robust understanding of their chosen industry, demonstrating a passion for the products and offering supreme quality and variety to captivate their target audience.

- Crafts and Handmade Goods Marketplaces

Platforms such as Etsy and Artfire excel in offering a space for artisans, crafters, and DIY enthusiasts to sell their handmade goods and supplies. These marketplaces foster creativity and individuality, showcasing unique and bespoke goods unavailable in traditional retail outlets.

Entrepreneurs considering this model need to appreciate and support artisans and their craft, nurturing a community spirit within their platform and placing their focus on authenticity and the stories behind the handmade items.

- Luxury Marketplaces

  Luxury marketplaces cater to the high-end consumer segment, offering premium products and services. Farfetch, for instance, specializes in luxury fashion, providing designer and limited edition clothing, accessories, and beauty products.

For entrepreneurs stepping into the realm of luxury marketplaces, the ability to cater to the refined tastes of discerning clientele, ensure top-notch quality, and provide exceptional customer service are key success factors.

- Hyperlocal Marketplaces

Hyperlocal marketplaces focus on a specific geographical location, catering to the needs of the local community. They offer services and products from businesses within a certain locality, which can range from food delivery, grocery shopping, home services, and more. Examples include Postmates and Instacart.

2.3 C2C (Consumer to Consumer)

C2C (Consumer to Consumer) online marketplaces have revolutionized the buying and selling dynamic by enabling direct transactions between consumers. These platforms allow individuals to sell goods or services to other individuals, fostering a peer-to-peer network that promotes reuse, affordability, and entrepreneurship.

As these marketplaces continue to expand and diversify, understanding the broad types within the C2C spectrum can provide crucial insights for entrepreneurs aspiring to venture into this realm.

Online Auction Sites

The online auction model is one of the earliest forms of C2C online marketplaces. Sites like eBay have made this format hugely popular, where consumers bid on items listed by other consumers. Sellers place a time limit on auctions, giving potential buyers the ability to offer their best price for the product.

Entrepreneurs interested in operating such a marketplace should consider creating mechanisms to ensure fair auctions, secure payments, and reliable shipping. It's also essential to forge a strong community of active users to maintain momentum and user interest.

Classified Ad Platforms

These marketplaces, such as Craigslist or Gumtree, operate similar to traditional newspaper classifieds, hosting advertisements for a range of products and services. They are often location-based, making them excellent for selling larger items like furniture or vehicles that are inconvenient to ship.

Entrepreneurs considering this model should focus on an easy-to-use ad setup, efficient search functionalities, and robust security protocols to safeguard transactions and users' personal information.

Used Goods Marketplaces

These marketplaces focus specifically on the resale of used items, promoting sustainability and affordability. Platforms like Poshmark and Depop cater to the fashion industry, focusing on used clothing, whereas Bookfinder is a dedicated platform for used books.

For entrepreneurs looking to start a used goods marketplace, it's essential to stress on the integrity of listed items, facilitate easy communication between buyers and sellers, and ensure secure payment and delivery methods.

Peer-to-Peer Services Platforms

These marketplaces connect consumers in need of certain services with other consumers who can provide these services. TaskRabbit, for example, pairs users with local contractors who can perform tasks like moving, cleaning, or minor repairs.

Entrepreneurs pursuing a peer-to-peer services marketplace must establish robust measures to verify the competence and trustworthiness of service providers. They must also offer an easy hiring process and secure payment options.

Crowdfunding Marketplaces

Platforms like Kickstarter or Indiegogo provide a marketplace for consumers to fund projects or ideas presented by other consumers. This provides creators a platform to realize their ideas and projects with collective funding.

Chapter three

Identifying your Niche and Creating a Unique Value Proposition

3.1 Finding the Perfect Niche

For an aspiring online marketplace entrepreneur, one of the key factors to achieve success in the competitive landscape is finding the perfect niche. Identifying the right niche involves a deep understanding of your target audience and creating a distinctive value proposition that caters to their specific needs. This approach not only helps you to cater to a particular market segment effectively but also enables you to distinguish your marketplace from competitors.

The following guidelines will assist you in identifying the perfect niche and crafting a compelling value proposition, providing the foundation for your online marketplace venture.

1. Market Research

Conducting comprehensive market research is the first step towards identifying a viable niche. This process involves analyzing industry trends, consumer behavior, and your competitors. Investigate the current landscape of the market to determine what types of marketplaces are in high demand, what pain points customers are facing, and possible gaps your platform could address.

2. Determine Your Passion and Expertise

Selecting a niche that aligns with your passion and expertise will increase your understanding of the particular industry and foster an authentic connection with your target audience. Your passion will translate into a commitment to serve your clientele, while your expertise will help you make informed decisions and ensure that your marketplace is consistent with industry standards and expectations.

3. Evaluate Market Viability and Profitability

After identifying a potential niche that resonates with your passion and skills, assess the market viability and profitability by considering factors such as target audience size, growth potential, and revenue projections. Determining the niche's sustainability and potential for profit ensures that your marketplace can thrive in the long run.

4. Assess the Competition

Analyze your competition within the chosen niche to understand their strengths, weaknesses, and provided offerings. Gain insights into how they have positioned themselves in the market and whether you can differentiate your platform from theirs. Identifying an angle to differentiate from the competition will help you establish a strong selling point and unique identity for your marketplace.

5. Define Your Unique Value Proposition

Crafting a unique value proposition (UVP) is essential to show your target audience why they should choose your platform over competing marketplaces. Your UVP should emphasize the key features and benefits of your platform that cater to the specific needs of your niche audience. Be clear, concise, and compelling in your messaging, and ensure that your UVP differentiates your platform from others in the market.

6. Test and Validate Your Idea

Finally, before diving headfirst into the development and launch of your marketplace, validate your idea by testing it with your target audience. Share your concept and UVP with them and solicit feedback to gauge potential interest, acceptance, and areas of improvement. Ensuring that your platform resonates with your target audience and addresses their needs will provide a strong foundation for its success.

3.2 Developing a Unique Value Proposition

In the vast digital marketplace terrain, developing a unique value proposition (UVP) can set your platform apart from competitors and bolster your niche identification strategy. A compelling UVP clarifies your marketplace's value and uniqueness, leading your brand to resonate with your identified niche.

Below are critical steps to follow when developing a unique value proposition for your online marketplace. This offers a guide on creating a UVP that speaks directly to your target audience's needs and preferences while distinguishing your platform amidst the competition.

Understand Your Audience

Before you start developing your UVP, you need to fully understand your target audience. Determine their needs, behaviours, preferences, and pain points. Conduct surveys or interviews to acquire firsthand insights into what they value in an online marketplace. Invest time in getting to know your potential customers, as this understanding forms the foundation for creating a effective value proposition.

Analyze Your Competitors

Perform a detailed competition analysis to understand the existing UVPs in your chosen niche. Evaluate your competitors' strengths, weaknesses, and overall strategies.

Unveil what they present as their value proposition and identify any gaps in their offerings. This will guide you in creating a proposition that differentiates your platform and offers distinctive features and benefits.

Identify and Articulate your Unique Strengths

Highlight and articulate the unique strengths and features your marketplace brings to the table. These could include better pricing, superior quality, exceptional service, innovative features, or an improved user experience. The identified unique strengths should answer the question, "Why should a customer choose our marketplace over the competitors?"

Develop a Clear and Compelling UVP

Keeping in mind the acquired insights about your audience, competition, and unique strengths, craft a precise, clear, and attractive UVP. It should succinctly and convincingly communicate how your platform offers superior value to your target audience. Ensure it resonates with your audience's interests, addresses their primary pain-points, and showcases your platform as an optimal solution to their needs.

Test, Validate, and Refine

Once you have developed your UVP, the next step is to test it with your target audience. Use A/B testing, customer interviews, or surveys to collect feedback, and gauge the effectiveness of your UVP. This step offers the opportunity to refine your value proposition according to the reactions and feedback from your prospective customers.

Communicate Your UVP Everywhere

Once your UVP is finalized, it should be effectively communicated across all your marketing and communication channels. This includes your website, social media platforms, email marketing campaigns, and any advertising or promotional efforts. Consistent messaging will amplify the reach and impact of your UVP.

Chapter four

Business Model of Online Marketplace

4.1 Various Models to Choose From

Choosing the right business model is a critical step in creating a successful online marketplace. The business model you choose will dictate how your platform generates revenue, interacts with users, and scales over time. This section explores various models of online marketplaces that entrepreneurs can choose from when launching their online marketplace venture.

1. Commission Model

   The commission model is the most common and straightforward business model for online marketplaces. Here, the marketplace brings buyers and sellers together and charges a fee (commission) for each successful transaction. This model is popular because it aligns with the platform's ability to bring value to its users. Examples include eBay, Etsy, and Amazon Marketplace.

2. Subscription Model

   In the subscription model, users pay a regular recurring fee to access the product or service. This model provides a predictable, recurring revenue stream for the marketplaces that adds stability. A prominent example is LinkedIn, where users pay for premium features.

3. Listing Fee Model

   In the listing fee model, sellers pay a fee to list their products or services on the marketplace. This model is beneficial when the marketplace has a large, active buyer base, making listings more valuable. Etsy, for example, charges a small listing fee per product in addition to its commission model.

4. Freemium Model

   The freemium model allows users to access basic features for free while charging for premium features. This model can be effective for attracting a large user base and prompting users to upgrade for added benefits. An example of a marketplace using the freemium model is Dropbox, where users have free storage up to a certain limit and can pay for additional storage.

5. Lead Generation Model

   The lead generation model suits service-oriented marketplaces where the platform charges service providers for connecting them with potential customers or leads. The platform may charge per lead or charge a subscription fee for access to a certain number of leads per month. Thumbtack is an example of a marketplace that uses the lead generation model.

6. Hybrid Model

   Some marketplaces implement a combination of the business models mentioned above to diversify their revenue streams. A marketplace may have a subscription model with added in-app purchases or use a commission model with a listing fee model. For instance, Etsy charges a listing fee and a transaction fee, displaying a hybrid model.

4.2 Exploring Revenue Streams

Developing multiple revenue streams is crucial to building a sustainable and thriving online marketplace. By diversifying your sources of income, you can mitigate risks associated with fluctuations in individual revenue streams and maximize your platform's profitability. This section examines various revenue streams that entrepreneurs can explore and integrate into their online marketplace's business model for sustainable growth.

1. Advertising and Sponsored Listings

    One way to diversify your income is by allowing businesses to advertise on your marketplace. You can offer paid banner ads, sponsored listings, or featured products that appear more prominently in search results for increased visibility. Decide whether to charge advertisers on a cost-per-impression (CPM) or a cost-per-click (CPC) basis as part of your monetization strategy.

2. Premium Features and Subscriptions

   Offering premium features or subscription plans can encourage users to pay for additional benefits not available to free users. This model often works well when basic services are offered for free, and more advanced features are available for a fee. Examples of premium features can include ad removal, faster customer support, enhanced customization options, and access to exclusive content or discounts.

3. Licensing or White Labeling

   If you have developed unique technology, software, or features for your marketplace, you may consider licensing or white labelling them to other organizations. Licensing allows you to charge a fee for others to use your technology while white labelling refers to selling your service as a turnkey solution, allowing others to rebrand it as their own.

4. Data Monetization

As your online marketplace grows, collecting valuable data on customer preferences, behaviours, and trends can be an asset. You can monetize this data (while remaining GDPR compliant and respecting user privacy) by selling it to third parties for research, marketing, or product development purposes.

5. Affiliate Programs

Partnering with other businesses through affiliate marketing programs can be an additional revenue stream. Collaborate with companies offering complementary products or services and earn a commission for each successful referral that results in a sale. This not only generates income but also expands your marketplace's offerings, increasing its overall value.

6. Coaching, Training, and Consulting Services

   If you have established expertise in your niche or marketplace development, consider offering coaching, training, or consulting services. This can expand your marketplace's value proposition while generating an additional revenue stream. You can offer these services as one-off packages or ongoing support for users looking to improve their online business ventures.

7. Strategic Partnerships or Integrations

   Developing strategic partnerships or integrations with other businesses, software, or tools can create further revenue opportunities. Through partnerships, you can offer special discounts, exclusive features, or access to complementary services, charging partner organizations for these promotional opportunities.

4.3 Pricing Strategy That Works

In the online marketplace business, deploying an appropriate and effective pricing strategy is a critical component of success. An optimally designed pricing strategy allows your platform to compete effectively, maximize revenues, and also create value for your users. This section explores how to craft a pricing strategy that works with your business model in an online marketplace setup.

Cost-Plus Pricing

Cost-plus pricing involves determining the cost of providing a service and adding an acceptable profit margin. While straightforward, this approach may fail to account for the complexities of market dynamics such as competition and value perception. Use this model with caution, ensuring that the final price aligns with customers' willingness to pay and doesn't exceed what competitors are charging for similar services.

Value-Based Pricing

In value-based pricing, the price is based on the perceived value of a product or service, rather than the actual cost of delivering it. This approach requires an intimate understanding of your customers and their perception of your platform's value. When correctly implemented, it can help your marketplace command higher prices and drive customer loyalty.

Competition-Based Pricing

In a highly competitive market, pricing your services similar to or slightly lower than your competitors can be an effective strategy. However, care should be taken not to embark on a race to the bottom, as this can erode profit margins and lead to the devaluation of your platform.

Dynamic Pricing

Dynamic pricing involves adjusting prices in real-time based on market demand, available supply, and other external factors. This model can maximize profits during peak times and ensure sales during slower periods. Marketplaces like Uber and Airbnb use dynamic pricing to balance supply and demand effectively.

Tiered Pricing

Offering multiple pricing tiers with varying levels of access or features can help appeal to a broader audience. Each tier should deliver added value proportionate to its price point. This way, customers can choose the one that best suits their needs and willingness to pay, while you generate revenue from a wider range of customers.

Freemium Pricing

The freemium model involves offering a basic version of your service for free, while charging for premium features or services. This model can help attract a large initial user base, some of whom may eventually convert to paying customers.

Psychological Pricing

Applying psychological principles to your pricing strategy can encourage purchases. Practices like setting prices slightly below a round number ($0.99 instead of $1, or $199 instead of $200) can make prices appear significantly lower in the eyes of customers, prompting more sales.

Chapter five

Building the Marketplace

5.1 Setting Up the Platform

Setting up a successful online marketplace entails rigorous planning, careful decision-making, and the use of powerful digital tools to ensure you meet the dynamic needs of both buyers and sellers. The initial setup of the platform underpins how effective the marketplace will be and how well it can adapt and scale as your business evolves. This section delves into the key stages involved in setting up the platform for your marketplace.

Understanding Your Target Audience

Before you begin building your platform, clearly define and understand your target audience, i.e., the key users who will drive your marketplace activities. This includes both buyers and sellers. Comprehensive audience research should take into consideration demographics, preferences, likes, dislikes, and behaviors. This helps to inform the platform's design, layout, usability, and functionality.

Choosing the Right Technology Stack

The next step is deciding on the technology stack that will drive your online marketplace. This can heavily influence the site's performance, scalability, and overall user experience. You can choose between custom development or a turnkey solution.

If you choose custom development, you have the flexibility to design and implement features suitably tailored to your marketplace needs. However, it demands more time and resources. Popular languages for backend development include Ruby, Python, and Java, while frontend development usually uses HTML, CSS, JavaScript, or their frameworks like React or Vue.js.

On the other hand, a turnkey solution like Sharetribe, Wix, or Shopify provides ready-made platforms that can be set up quickly, but with limited customization.

Designing an Intuitive User Interface (UI)

Your UI is the first point of contact between users and your marketplace. Designing an intuitive, easy-to-use UI can streamline the user experience, making it easier for users to navigate and ensuring they can find what they need with minimal hassle. Important elements to consider include site navigation, layout, color schemes, typography, and more.

Implementing Essential Features

Certain features drive the functionality of any online marketplace. These include user profiles, product listings, search and filter functions, payment processing, reviews and ratings, and a robust, secure checkout process. Depending upon the niche and requirements, you may also consider implementing advanced features like geolocation, notifications, instant chat, and personalized recommendations.

Ensuring Robust Security

Security should be a top priority when setting up the platform. A secure marketplace builds trust with your users. Ensure SSL encryption, secure payment processing, data privacy, and regular security updates to keep user data safe.

Testing & Quality Assurance

Before launching, thorough testing and quality assurance checks are crucial to ensure that all features work as expected and the user experience is seamless. This should involve functionality testing, usability testing, performance testing, and security testing.

5.2 UI/UX Design for Enhancing User Experience

A well-designed user interface (UI) and user experience (UX) are vital for enhancing the value of your online marketplace. Intuitive and user-friendly design helps retain users, drives engagement, and ultimately generates sales and revenue. This section presents key aspects of crafting UI/UX designs that maximize the usability, accessibility, and charm of your marketplace platform, contributing to its success.

User-Centered Design Approach

Taking a user-centered design approach ensures that your marketplace satisfies the specific needs of your target audience. Gather user data through research, surveys, and observations to create personas representing different customer segments. Utilize these personas to inform design decisions, ensuring that the platform appeals to your intended audience.

Consistent Design Language

Consistency in design elements like color schemes, typography, icons, and layouts helps create a cohesive and professional appearance. Establish a design system to serve as a guideline for the look and feel of your marketplace, contributing to overall branding and user familiarity.

Simple and Intuitive Navigation

A straightforward and intuitive navigation structure is crucial for providing a seamless user experience. Users should be able to quickly identify and access the required sections or actions. Consider implementing a clear top-level navigation menu, breadcrumbs, and clearly visible calls to action (CTAs) to facilitate smooth user flow throughout the platform.

Visual Hierarchy and Layout

Crafting a visual hierarchy in your design can help guide users to important elements and actions. Employ layout techniques like grid systems or card-based designs, and use typography, colours, contrast, and white space effectively, making it easy for users to focus on key sections of the platform and perform actions with minimal cognitive load.

Engagement through Personalization

Connect with users by incorporating personalization elements into your UI/UX design, such as displaying recommended products or utilizing past user history to make tailored suggestions. Personalized experiences can boost user engagement, prompt return visits, and give your platform a competitive edge.

Responsive Design

With users accessing your platform through various devices, ensuring your design is responsive is crucial to delivering a consistent and optimal experience across different screen sizes. Employing responsive designs that adapt to mobile devices, tablets, and desktops can improve overall accessibility and user satisfaction.

Usability Testing and Iteration

Implement usability testing with a diverse mix of users to identify areas for improvement or potential pain points. The feedback gathered should be used to iterate and refine your UI/UX design accordingly, ensuring that the design continuously optimizes the user experience.

Accessibility for All Users

Design your marketplace platform with accessibility in mind, enabling users of varying abilities to access, understand, and interact with your platform. Follow accessibility guidelines such as Web Content Accessibility Guidelines (WCAG) to ensure your marketplace can accommodate the largest possible user base.

5.3 Legal Aspects to Consider

Setting up an online marketplace involves much more than just the technological and design aspects; it also requires careful consideration of various legal issues. Balancing your marketplace's business needs with legal compliance can help avoid costly lawsuits, fines, and damage to your reputation. This section focuses on the significant legal aspects you need to consider when building your marketplace.

Business Registration

Choosing the right business structure and registering your company is the first legal step. This can have implications for tax, liability, and management of your marketplace. Options range from sole proprietorships and partnerships to corporations and limited liability companies.

Intellectual Property Protection

Consider copyright, trademark, and patent laws to protect your marketplace's unique features, brand name, logo, and any innovative technology or anticipated technology advancements you develop.

Privacy Policy and Terms of Use

A privacy policy is a legal requirement for any online marketplace that collects user data. It states how you gather, store, and use customer data, which is crucial in the era of data breaches and privacy concerns. Terms of use set ground rules for how your site is used. You should clearly outline user rights and responsibilities, disclaimers, and limitations of liability.

Data Protection and Security

In line with privacy policies, enforce solid data protection measures to comply with regulations like the General Data Protection Regulation (GDPR) in the EU and the California Consumer Privacy Act (CCPA) in the US. Having secure measures against potential security threats further reinforces trust with your customers.

eCommerce Regulations

Your marketplace needs to adhere to specific eCommerce regulations designated by local, national, and international laws. These regulations may cover areas such as online advertising, consumer protection, digital transactions, and more.

Tax Compliance

Your marketplace must follow tax laws applicable to your geographic location and where your customers reside. This includes sales tax, VAT, and income tax. Detailed records of all sales transactions, including invoices, should be kept for tax purposes.

Licensing and Permits

Depending on the nature of the products or services traded on your platform, you may require various licenses or permits. For instance, real estate, food, or healthcare marketplaces may have specific licensing requirements.

Vendor Agreement

If third-party vendors will be selling products or services through your marketplace, have a comprehensive agreement outlining their obligations, commission rates, and stipulations around issues like returns and customer disputes.

Employment Laws

If you plan on hiring employees or freelancers, you'll need to stay compliant with labour laws, which cover issues like minimum wage, overtime, benefits, and workplace safety.

Chapter six

Marketing and Acquiring Users

6.1 Essential Digital Marketing Strategies

A successful online marketplace requires effective marketing strategies that draw in both buyers and sellers, ensuring a thriving, competitive ecosystem. Properly executed digital marketing tactics can raise awareness, generate interest, and convert potential users into loyal customers. This section will examine the essential digital marketing strategies to bolster the marketing and acquisition efforts for your online marketplace.

Search Engine Optimization (SEO)

SEO is pivotal for driving organic traffic to your marketplace. By optimizing your platform's content and structure, you can achieve higher search engine rankings, resulting in increased visibility. This includes keyword research, on-page optimization, quality content production, and improving the site's technical foundation, such as load speed, mobile-friendliness, and security.

Pay-Per-Click (PPC) Advertising

PPC ads offer a cost-effective way to target specific audience segments and instantly drive traffic to your marketplace. Platforms like Google Ads and Bing Ads enable you to bid on keywords and get your ads displayed on search engine results pages (SERPs) or within display networks.

Social Media Marketing

Leveraging social media platforms like Facebook, Twitter, Instagram, LinkedIn, and Pinterest can expand your marketplace's reach and improve audience engagement. Share quality content, promotions, and updates regularly, while fostering community and interacting with users in a genuine, helpful manner. Social media ads and influencer partnerships can also attract potential users.

Content Marketing

Content marketing involves creating, curating, and sharing high-quality, informative, or entertaining content that appeals to your target audience. Blog posts, articles, videos, infographics, or podcasts which address relevant topics and resonate with users can drive website visits and generate qualified leads. A well-executed content marketing strategy can position your marketplace as a trusted authority and resource in your niche.

Email Marketing

Email marketing remains one of the most potent and cost-effective marketing channels. Build a targeted email list and use it to share helpful content, special offers, and updates, maintaining regular communication with your audience. Personalized, segmented, and automated email campaigns can help nurture prospects and lead them toward conversion.

Affiliate Marketing

Collaborating with affiliates or partners can extend your marketplace's reach and generate new leads. Affiliates promote your marketplace in exchange for a commission on sales or leads their efforts generate.

Online Events and Webinars

Hosting online events, workshops, or webinars relevant to your marketplace's niche can attract potential users and demonstrate your expertise. This format also offers interactive opportunities, such as Q&A sessions, in which you can directly address user concerns and highlight your marketplace's value proposition.

Analyzing and Measuring Success

Track and analyze marketing efforts using analytics tools like Google Analytics or specific platform metrics to evaluate the effectiveness of your strategies. Based on the data, iterate and optimize your marketing efforts continuously to maximize ROI.

6.2 Advertisement and PR

To build a strong user base for your online marketplace, you need to raise awareness, establish credibility, and generate interest among potential buyers and sellers. Robust advertising and public relations (PR) strategies play a pivotal role in accomplishing these goals. The following sections delve into effective advertising and PR tactics that contribute to the successful marketing and acquisition of users for your online marketplace.

Advertising Methods for Marketplaces

Advertising can boost your marketplace's visibility, drive user acquisition, and encourage conversions. Explore different advertising mediums to reach and resonate with your target audience.

Display Advertising

Display advertising involves placing visual ads on websites, social media platforms, and apps, reaching potential users while they browse the internet. With a compelling design and a clear value proposition, display ads can increase brand awareness and generate leads. Consider programmatic advertising and retargeting to optimize and refine your display ad strategy.

Video Advertising

Video ads on platforms such as YouTube or Facebook can create an emotional connection with your audience, showcase your marketplace's features, and provide engaging storytelling opportunities. Leverage these ads to reach audiences that consume more video content and prefer visual communication.

Native Advertising

Native ads integrate with the content and design of a host website or platform, offering a less intrusive experience for users. Platforms like Taboola and Outbrain enable you to place your marketplace's content on highly trafficked websites, increasing your exposure to potential users.

Social Media Advertising

Social media platforms offer advertising solutions to reach precise segments of your target audience. Ads on platforms like Facebook, Instagram, LinkedIn, and Twitter can drive traffic, foster engagement, and help with user acquisition initiatives.

PR Tactics for Marketplaces

Public relations can help build your marketplace's credibility and generate positive buzz. A well-executed PR campaign can attract organic attention, ultimately resulting in word-of-mouth marketing and an enhanced brand reputation.

Press Releases

Distribute press releases to relevant media outlets, bloggers, and influencers to announce noteworthy events (e.g., launches, milestones, or partnerships) in your online marketplace. A well-crafted press release can spark interest and lead to media coverage, increasing your marketplace's visibility.

Media Outreach and Coverage

Forge relationships with influential journalists, bloggers, and writers in your niche and develop story ideas to pitch. Media features, interviews, guest posts, or contributed articles can position your marketplace as an industry leader and reach new customers.

Influencer Partnerships

Collaborate with trusted influencers in your marketplace's domain. Partnerships, endorsements, or sponsored content can increase awareness, enhance credibility, and tap into the influencer's established audience.

Community Engagement

Participate in or host industry events, conferences, webinars, or workshops to connect with your target audience, strengthen your brand identity, and foster community growth. Actively engage in online forums, industry groups, and social media platforms to further cultivate a sense of belonging and trust.

Crisis Communication

Prepare a crisis communication plan to protect your marketplace's reputation in case of unforeseen events, such as security breaches, platform outages, or negative press. Swift, transparent communication and proactive problem-solving can mitigate damage and safeguard user trust.

6.3 Leveraging Social Influencers

Influencer marketing has become a powerful tool for businesses, with social influencers potentially driving user engagement and acquisition in a way few other marketing strategies can. By leveraging influencers, online marketplaces can forge stronger connections with their audiences and enhance brand credibility through personalization and authentic storytelling. This section discusses how to leverage social influencers effectively for marketing and acquiring users for your online marketplace.

Understanding Influencer Marketing

Influencer marketing involves collaborating with influencers – individuals with a significant social media following or known authority in a specific niche – to promote your online marketplace. The influencer may use a variety of media, such as blog posts or social media content, to share experiences or insights about your platform, making their followers more likely to try your marketplace.

Identifying The Right Influencers

Choosing the right influencers is crucial for the success of your influencer marketing campaign. The ideal influencer should align with your brand's values, have a follower base that matches your target audience, and wield the power to engage and influence their followers. Tools such as BuzzSumo, Klear, or Upfluence can simplify the process of finding suitable influencers.

Nurturing Relationships with Influencers

Once you have identified potential influencers, begin to foster a relationship. Engage with their content, show appreciation for their work, and propose collaboration in a personalized way. Honesty, respect, and patience are crucial elements in building a long-term mutually beneficial partnership.

Collaborating with Influencers

How influencers promote your marketplace will depend on their channel, style, and audience. Bloggers might write a detailed review, Instagram influencers could share product photos, YouTubers might create an unboxing or walkthrough video, or podcast hosts could interview a representative from your marketplace. The content should come across as genuine and align with the influencer's usual content to maintain authenticity.

Tracking and Measuring Success

After launching an influencer campaign, it's essential to track its performance. You can use metrics such as engagement rate, impressions, reach, click-throughs, and conversions. Tools like Google Analytics and UTM parameters can offer valuable insights.

Influencer Marketing and User Acquisition Strategy

Integrating influencer marketing into your existing user acquisition strategy can be highly beneficial. Influencers provide social proof, compelling storytelling, and a personalized connection that can be more effective than traditional advertising in capturing attention and driving platform sign-ups.

Chapter Seven

Scaling your Online Marketplace

7.1 Advanced Marketing Strategies for Growth

As your online marketplace matures and the user base expands, your marketing strategy should evolve as well. At this stage, your focus should shift to not just acquire new users, but also towards retaining existing customers, driving revenue, and fostering sustainable growth. This section outlines advanced marketing strategies for scaling an online marketplace.

Expansion into New Segments

One way to fuel growth is by tapping into new market segments. Research and identify potential areas where your marketplace can cater to a new or underserved audience. This could involve introducing new product lines, targeting a different demographic, or expanding geographically.

Data-Driven Marketing

Leveraging data and analytics helps make informed decisions, refine marketing strategies, and optimize returns. Use data tools to gain insights about user behaviour, conversion rates, churn, customer lifetime value (CLTV), and more. By understanding these metrics, you can identify opportunities for growth and optimize your marketing efforts for maximum impact.

Lifecycle Marketing

Consider the lifecycle of your users and tailor marketing strategies to each stage. Lead nurturing campaigns can pull new users into the marketplace. Onboarding campaigns can help new users find value in your marketplace faster. Retention emails and personalized offers can keep users engaged, while reactivation campaigns can lure back inactive users.

Community Building

Foster a strong sense of community among your users. An engaged community can drive user retention, organic growth, and brand loyalty. Use social media, blog posts, webinars, user engagement events, and forums to build and nurture these relationships.

Strategic Partnerships

Forming strategic partnerships can accelerate growth by giving you access to a broader customer base, complementary resources, or new markets. Collaborate with businesses that share your target audience but are not direct competitors.

Referral Programs

Leverage the power of word-of-mouth marketing with a referral program. Encourage your loyal users to invite others to your platform by offering incentives such as discounts, points, or cashback.

Advanced SEO Techniques

At an advanced stage, simple on-page SEO might not be enough. Consider incorporating more advanced SEO techniques like creating an XML sitemap, developing a link-building strategy, or optimizing your site structure for better crawling.

Diversifying Advertising Channels

Try out non-traditional platforms or advertising channels like podcast ads, collaborations with influencers or content creators, affiliate marketing, or TV ads. These can help you reach new audiences and reduce your dependence on a single advertising platform.

7.2 Partnering and Strategic Alliances

Online marketplaces can accelerate growth by leveraging strategic partnerships and alliances to amplify their reach, strengthen their service offerings, and gain competitive advantages. This section discusses various aspects of partnering and forming strategic alliances for scaling your online marketplace.

Types of Strategic Partnerships

Strategic partnerships can take several forms, depending on your business objectives and the nature of your partners. Some popular types of strategic alliances include:

Co-marketing Partnerships

Online marketplaces can collaborate with complementary businesses to create joint marketing campaigns, cross-promoting each other's platforms, or offering bundled products and services that appeal to their shared target audience.

Channel Partnerships

Online marketplaces can partner with channel partners to expand their reach into new geographic locations or verticals, boost visibility, and drive user acquisition. Channel partnerships can involve wholesalers, retailers, agencies, or affiliates who help promote the marketplace to their clientele or network.

Product Integration Partnerships

Collaborating with other businesses to integrate their products or services into your online marketplace can enhance its overall value proposition. Product integrations can streamline user experience, drive customer satisfaction, and distinguish your marketplace from competitors.

Technology Partnerships

Forming alliances with technology partners can help your marketplace leverage cutting-edge solutions, drive innovation, and increase scalability. Technology partners can provide robust tools, expertise, or infrastructure, further fueling the growth of your online marketplace.

Benefits of Strategic Partnerships

Strategic partnerships can have several advantages for your online marketplace. Some benefits include:

1. Access to new audiences: Strategic partners can introduce your platform to their existing customer

base or social network, driving user acquisition and expanding market reach.

2. Increased credibility and trust: By association with established brands, your marketplace can instantly gain credibility and instill more trust in potential users.

3. Shared resources and cost savings: Collaborating with partners on marketing efforts, technology development, or customer support can lead to shared resources, saving time and reducing costs.

4. Enhanced innovation and problem-solving: Combining complementary skills, expertise, and experiences can drive innovation and creative problem-solving, making your marketplace more competitive in the market.

How to Form Strategic Partnerships

To identify and form successful strategic alliances, follow these steps:

1. Set clear objectives: Determine your priorities and goals for the partnership. This clarity will help you identify the ideal partner and craft an effective partnership strategy.

2. Research potential partners: Identify businesses with complementary offerings, shared values, and a target audience that overlaps with that of your marketplace.

3. Network: Attend industry events, conferences, or trade shows to meet potential partners, engage with them, and create a rapport before proposing a partnership.

4. Present a win-win proposition: Develop a partnership proposal highlighting mutual benefits,

ensuring that both parties stand to gain from the collaboration.

5. Define roles and responsibilities: Once the partnership is established, outline each party's roles, responsibilities, and expectations to avoid misunderstandings and ensure smooth collaboration.

6. Measure success: Establish key performance indicators (KPIs) and metrics to track the partnership's success and make data-driven adjustments as required.

7.3 Expanding into New Markets

Market expansion is a strategic move towards growing your online marketplace and, consequently, your revenue and user base. Moving into new markets could mean diversifying your product or service range, reaching new customer demographics, or expanding geographically. This section will explore effective strategies for expanding your online marketplace into new markets.

Identifying New Market Opportunities

Before expanding, it's crucial to identify markets where your marketplace can thrive. Market research should take precedence, including competitive analysis to recognize gaps your marketplace can fill. Utilize tools like Google Trends and Surveys, Statista, Pew Research Center, and industry-specific reports to gather information about your potential markets.

Test and Validate the New Market

Before fully diving in, conduct pilot tests or initial launches in the new market to gauge reception. Use the MVP (Minimum Viable Product) principle to experiment with a basic version of your proposition and collect data on market receptiveness. This will help mitigate potential risks and guide your full-scale approach.

Localization for New Markets

If you're expanding into a different region or country, ensure your marketplace is culturally relevant and sensitive, linguistically accurate, and satisfies all local legal compliance requirements. Localization goes beyond translation and includes price adjustments, addressing regional preferences and cultural nuances, accommodating local payment methods, and ensuring proper customer service support.

Develop a Go-to-Market (GTM) Strategy

A GTM strategy is a comprehensive plan outlining how you will sell your product or service to customers in the new market. It typically covers pricing strategies, sales and distribution models, marketing and advertising plans, and a clear list of action items and milestones to measure your progress.

Marketing and Promotion

Define a local marketing strategy to create a buzz around your marketplace. This may involve influencer marketing, partnerships with local businesses, attending local events, PPC advertising, SEO adjustments to rank in local search results, or even a dedicated country-specific website or app.

Partner with Local Businesses or Influencers

Forming local alliances can offer immense benefits. Local partners understand the ecosystem much better, can provide invaluable guidance on consumer behavior, and may already have an existing customer base, which can be beneficial when launching a marketplace in a new area.

Monitor Performance and Make Iterative Improvements

Don't expect things to be perfect from the get-go. Collect feedback, continuously monitor your performance, and adjust your strategies based on results. Utilize analytics to measure the success of the expansion.

Chapter eight

Overcoming Challenges in Scaling

8.1 Problem-solving for Common Issues

As your online marketplace grows and scales, you will undoubtedly encounter challenges. From managing an ever-growing user base to dealing with technical hiccups to embracing regulatory changes, every stage of scaling presents unique hurdles. However, by anticipating these issues and developing effective problem-solving strategies, you can overcome these challenges and maintain steady growth.

Managing Increased Demand and User Expectations

As your user base grows, so does the demand for your services and the expectations of your consumers.

Problem-solving Strategy:

Invest in scalable infrastructure and resources to handle the increased load. Enhance your customer service team, implement robust automation tools to speed up processes, and use feedback systems to continually improve service quality.

Maintaining Service Quality

Keeping the quality of services high while scaling can be a challenge, especially when dealing with multiple sellers or service providers.

Problem-solving Strategy:

Implement rigorous seller vetting processes to maintain service quality. Use ratings and reviews to track seller performance. Offer training and support to sellers to help them improve their services.

Scaling Customer Support

As you scale, you might face challenges in maintaining a high level of customer support.

Problem-solving Strategy:

Invest in customer support technology like chatbots, AI-assisted support, and automated helpdesk systems. Create a comprehensive FAQ or help center where users can find answers to their queries. Consider outsourcing or augmenting your customer support team during peak demand times.

Regulatory Compliance

Expansion into new markets often means dealing with different regulatory environments and compliance issues.

Problem-solving Strategy:

Stay abreast with the local regulatory landscape with the help of legal advisors. Prepare for regulatory changes by building compliant processes and ensuring data privacy and security.

Maintaining Site Performance and Uptime

A rapidly growing user base, increased transactions, and growing data might increase the load on your technology infrastructure, leading to performance issues or downtime.

Problem-solving Strategy:

Opt for scalable hosting solutions, invest in failover systems, and have a robust disaster recovery plan in place. Regularly audit your site performance and proactively address performance bottlenecks.

Balancing Growth and Profitability

Many marketplaces struggle to strike the right balance between driving growth and managing costs.

Problem-solving Strategy:

Fine-tune your revenue model, focusing on profitable growth. Leverage data to understand the cost-to-value ratio of different business activities and optimize accordingly. Consider different monetization strategies like premium listings, subscription fees, or tiered commission structures.

Conclusion

Building and scaling an e-commerce platform is an exciting and challenging adventure. It is a journey that's not only propelled by innovative ideas and technology but also strongly influenced by a deep understanding of customer behaviour, market dynamics, and an agile spirit of adaptability.

The process starts with identifying a profitable niche, conducting rigorous market research, and crafting a distinct value proposition. From gathering product listings or services to attracting the first users, the startup phase is all about setting the stage for future growth.

Next comes the journey towards growth and scaling up, which may involve expanding into new markets, integrating advanced technologies, and nurturing strategic partnerships. As the platform grows, the focus intensifies on maintaining service quality, providing excellent customer care, and dealing with regulatory compliance. This underscores the importance of building a robust foundation, scalable operations, and agile problem-solving mechanisms.

Entrepreneurs face challenges throughout this voyage. From competitive pressure to managing user expectations, scaling customer support to maintaining site performance, handling these growing pains can be daunting. However, overcoming these issues through innovative problem-solving strategies is where the real art of the entrepreneur shines.

While the idea of creating a successful online marketplace is glamorous, it requires unflagged commitment, a deep understanding of the target market, and the ability to anticipate and adapt to change. It's about exploring every avenue of potential growth while creating and maintaining a rich, user-friendly experience.

Above all, the ethos of a successful marketplace entrepreneur encapsulates the spirit of service. This journey is ultimately about creating a platform that provides immense value to all stakeholders - buyers, sellers, and partners alike. A successful online marketplace is not merely a place to conduct transactions, but a flourishing community where users' needs are consistently met and often exceeded.